Life Hacks for Cats

OR HOW TO TRAIN YOUR HUMAN

Life Hacks for Cats

OR HOW TO TRAIN YOUR HUMAN

BY BEAN THE TONKINESE

(AND PENNED BY GRANT DYSON) • ILLUSTRATED BY ROSS HAMILTON

BATEMAN BOOKS

Text © Grant Dyson, 2021
Illustrations © Ross Hamilton, 2021
Typographical design © David Bateman Ltd, 2021

Published in 2021 by David Bateman Ltd
2/5 Workspace Drive, Hobsonville, Auckland 0618, New Zealand
www.batemanbooks.co.nz

ISBN 978-1-98-853867-9

Book design: Cheryl Smith, Macarn Design.
Printed in China by Everbest Investment Ltd.

Contents

Hello, Fellow Felines!

As a smart Tonkinese (I like to think of myself as a scaled-down cheetah), with a face as dark as a bar of Whittaker's chocolate, I have become quite specialised in figuring out how to get the best from humans (an oddly hairless, flighty and unpredictable species) via careful nurturing and training. In recent years it has become apparent to me that I had a duty to pass on some of the life hacks I've learned along the way to my fellow felines, right down to the scruffiest moggy kitten. And so the idea for this book was born.

Some of the wildest stray cats who have been living rough will tell you 'never trust a human'. However, it may interest you to know that the two-legged species can in fact be trained to become surprisingly good . . .

companions. Note that I chose that word carefully — I didn't say servants. You have to pick the right humans, of course, and recognise that while animal traits sit just below the surface, a lot of how they behave comes down to strong herding instincts. Their species has fiercely dominant younger animals called influencers who lead the others.

So how exactly did I end up putting paw to paper and setting out to pass on some life hacks to my fellow felines? Actually there were no pens or paper, this being the 21st century after all. It was all electronic. And yet, naturally, paws are completely useless when it comes to typing on a keyboard. That's where G (short for Grant) came in. I'm his owner, and he's an incredibly well-trained pet, though he would probably say something different. He is quite old, tall with greying fur and a big nose, and is what some people call a 'cat lover'. His chosen mate R (short for Reta) is smaller, almost as old, and also with sparse grey fur. My name, Bean, is a reference to the luxurious coffee colour of my coat that I'm sure G believes is highly original. Nevertheless, I've grown very fond of the name.

So, I coerced G into becoming my scribe and assisting me in the education of my fellow felines. It's no secret that cats today are in dire need of sensible advice. So many end up in appalling circumstances after picking the wrong humans, with attempts to train the hairless beasts all in vain.

Thus, over a period of some months, G loyally typed out all my catty learnings: how to choose your human, how to interpret cat speak, basic techniques for getting the most pats, dos and don'ts. He hasn't censored anything, it's all my own words.

Don't believe the cynical strays: a good human is worth his or her weight in cat biscuits. But as I've said, choosing the right one is crucial. In *Life Hacks for Cats* I've described some of the archetypal humans who make the best companions. Don't believe anyone who tells you that dogs have owners, and that cats have staff. Basically, a bunch of dogs put that bit of fake news out there. They're always pushing that old 'man's best friend' line. Truth is, they know how well we've done on the internet in recent years, and they resent it. #catsofinstagram

Anyway, after some careful moulding G and R became the perfect cat companions. Greying old humans in their sixties are a great choice for a start. If they don't have grandchildren, cute and cuddly furry animals make excellent substitutes. Somehow, I even became R's dance partner. Read on, kittens, and learn everything you need to know in order to tame your human effectively.

Yours affectionately,

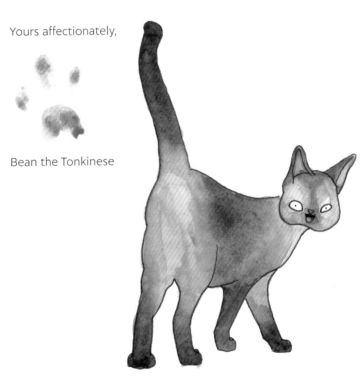

Bean the Tonkinese

A Note About Humans

Let's be clear from the start: humans are difficult and rather flighty animals, and thus they present some real challenges for any cat attempting to train them. They began as hunter-gatherers, but most have slipped out of hunting habits. However, given that hunting instincts are still present in many humans, even if deeply buried, you would expect them to have more sympathy for our own efforts. Don't make this mistake — they will often react badly when prey is placed proudly in front of them, but more on this later.

It is unfortunate but all cats must come to terms with some historic facts about humans, regardless of how kind and benevolent they may appear. The species has sat arrogantly at the top of the food chain for decades, and has a deeply ingrained sense of entitlement and superiority. Cats, like many other mammals, have suffered from humankind's attempts to impose its will on four-legged creatures.

Through the centuries there have been examples of humans committing the unspeakable: felinicide. They have branded us as 'feral' for the sake of their own particular agendas, such as the conservation of birds and other wildlife, conveniently forgetting their own role in wildlife devastation.

Cats like Tibbles have given the rest of us a bad name. She travelled with her owner, lighthouse keeper David Lyall, to an isolated island south of New Zealand in the late 1800s. There, she single-pawedly caused the extinction of the Stephens Island wren — a small, flightless bird. Though historians dispute that it was Tibbles alone who caused this rapid extinction, she nevertheless became the poster cat for our supposedly 'savage' nature.

Then there are the dark days of 1700s France, during which The Great Cat Massacre took place. Cats

were presumed to be 'possessed' (no doubt because of our almost supernatural suppleness) and the biggest felinicide in French history was committed.

Sadly, such attacks are not quite a thing of the past. Anti-cat crusaders have trapped and shot us in countries worldwide. Only animal rights activists have consistently treated animals as equals, rather than unintelligent beings to be dominated and subdued, if not eaten.

Eaten? Yes, I know. In Europe, where humans and animals have lived alongside each other for centuries, many used to turn to eating cat and dog meat when they ran out of other food. In Switzerland there have been several attempts as recent as the 1990s to ban

the barbaric rural practice of eating cats and dogs, but these attempts have failed.

Of course, humans have their cat-loving side too. The Egyptians idolised us for centuries, treating us with the reverence we deserve. They began regarding their cats as important members of their families and treated them with as much respect and dignity as their own children.

A modern version of this great veneration can be found in the cat cafés of Japan, in cities like Tokyo, with a population of nearly fourteen million humans, where pampered felines have a very high status. Cats are 'cute' and the Japanese are big fans of said cuteness.

They apply this aesthetic to anything, from comic book characters to cellphone attachments, even constructing a major brand inspired by cats — Hello Kitty. As a lifestyle fact, pets are out of reach to many in this crowded society, with apartment dwellers banned from keeping domestic animals. So, cat cafés give apartment dwellers, and cat lovers in general, a place to go and happily interact with us. Oh, imagine the many pats those cats must receive!

Cats have delighted humans in the media for many years. Garfield was an early trailblazer, an American comic strip that started in the 70s. Simon's Cat is an animated series based on the antics of a mischievous fat white cat and his owner Simon. That YouTube series has more than five million subscribers.

So, that, my furry friends, is a brief introduction to humans. Some of them are far easier to train to be friendly, accommodating and attentive food providers than others, which you really don't want to have to learn the hard way, believe me. In summary my good kittens, please read on and pay close attention to the following chapters, for in them I have summarised a lifetime's worth of human-wrangling wisdom just for you.

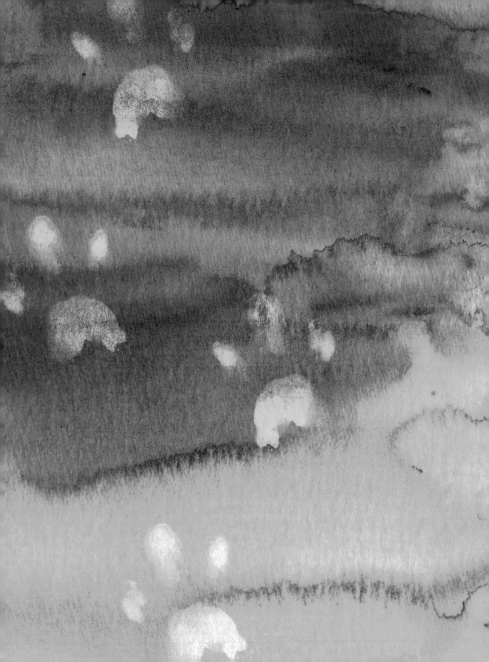

Understanding Humans

Humans are a strange species in many ways; they retain all sorts of animal traits and behaviours that lie just under the surface much of the time, hidden as they go about their modern lives. They can be intelligent and intuitive, and at times appear to display very cat-like emotions of fear, hunger and lust. Human behaviour varies enormously from person to person but, in general, it goes against their unwritten herding rules to display any of these emotions too openly. They apply phrases like 'bad manners', 'over the top' or 'a bit wild' to others who are free with their emotions.

Humans tend to lack a cat's Zen-like approach to life and never seem able to relax completely. They can become stressed to the point where they snap, and cats would do well to look out for any warning signs, as humans can become very dangerous under these circumstances. You'll see this stress when their faces look tight and almost dog-like, as if they are ready to snarl like a Dobermann. Given our innate expertise in relaxation, it's a cat's duty to help their human relax whenever possible, and humans have even studied how good we are at this.

Cats invented what humans came to call 'yoga' (though it should really have been 'catga') after studying our uniquely beneficial methods of stretching and contorting our bodies. In fact, its widely written that owning a cat helps to relieve stress and anxiety and can reduce the risk of heart attacks and strokes by more than a third. Yes, these facts may seem obvious to us, but humans are a cautious sort and require evidence provided by their chosen ambassadors of the truth.

Now that we've got our heads around humans a little better, we can focus on choosing the right human and training them with some particular tried and true methods like the 'nudge and rub' and the 'tap tap'. Some of these methods may seem unusual, but they work!

Pick Your Humans Carefully

Some of the best humans — that is, those most receptive to training — are couples without children, singles and the ones who are over 65 (did I mention that humans live absurdly long?). The latter category of human is also known as 'the elderly'.

Couples without children usually respond well to training. Human young (known as 'kids') are a time-consuming distraction for the humans who raise them. They are more helpless for longer than any other mammal, requiring a huge amount of feeding, dressing and looking after in general. And these children pose a constant risk where we cats are concerned. One minute a child can be sweetly stroking your coat, the next they are viciously pulling your tail! The unpredictable nature of these small humans means a cat can never put their trust in them until they reach the age of about ten. At that age their parents can finally start typical reward-based training: 'Can you put out the cat's dinner please, Johnny? I've got a treat for you if you help me,' etc.

Older children, especially teenagers, can in fact be very kind to cats and, if you give them enough affection, can be trained to provide you with treats. Some even aspire to work with animals in a zoo or a vet clinic. These particular humans will treat cats with almost as much reverence and affection as the ancient

Egyptians. If you have patience, the investment in a couple with children can pay off.

But couples without kids have been known to treat their pets like the children they never had. These humans will lavish affection on you, allowing you a prime spot on the sofa, and giving you the finest cuts of meat or choice fish to eat. They are more forgiving when it comes to a cat's 'bad' habits, like digging a hole in the vegetable garden to poo in. (How was I supposed to know it was their foraging ground?) They can afford to be more accommodating because their home is not in the state of messiness and turmoil that young humans produce.

Single humans can also be an excellent choice. Male or female, they can be alone for various reasons, including a deep devotion to this thing they call 'work'. A career-minded human can make a very good companion, so long as they put out your preferred food before leaving for 'work', and again on returning home. These people are often grateful for a purring, furry friend who makes few demands other than to sit on their lap while they watch Netflix.

Speaking of Netflix, have you seen *#CATS_The_Mewvie*? It should be required viewing for any human you are trying to train.

Older people, like G and R, make great cat staff — I mean . . . friends. (Note: Always use the term 'friends'.) Usually their children have grown up and left home so they have few distractions.

Some of them, like R, are desperately waiting for grandchildren to be born. In these cases, a cat can act as something of a human baby substitute and have all sorts of attention lavished upon it. Some people dress their pets up like human babies in hats and clothes, which I'm sure goes against the Universal Declaration of Cat Rights. R dressed me in a human baby's knitted hat once — I looked ridiculous. I humoured her briefly then tore it off. 'Oldies' like R are very receptive to training and can be taught to play games, but they can often take things too far. Occasionally, for example, R loves to pick me up and dance with me in the lounge, especially when certain flamenco-style music plays. I certainly don't remember consenting to this, and I sometimes get dizzy whirling around as she squeezes my head to her face, swaying back and forth. But it can be necessary to tolerate such ordeals if you want to keep your humans happy, and thankfully it doesn't usually last too long. I admit that sometimes I gaze helplessly at G who is always amused by the two of us dancing but pretends

to disapprove. He says things like: 'What are you doing to that poor cat?' R takes no notice.

Beware of cohabiting with scruffy young males who drive noisy cars and drink copious amounts of the liquid known as 'alcohol' (like catnip for humans). Not all males make bad companions, of course, but this type is sometimes known for mistreating animals. They often have bad-tempered dogs that love to chase us.

But, back to more pleasant topics. With our analysis of the different types of humans complete, I can now share with you my tips for training your new 'friends', beginning with attaining affection.

The Nudge and Rub Method

The 'nudge and rub' is one of the most basic of affectionate cat behaviours and your human can easily be taught how to participate. The most perceptive of them will pick up the technique from simply mimicking us. The best way to teach them is to jump up onto a chair or bench, anywhere that gives you access to their upper bodies. First, butt gently into their arm or shoulder and, if they respond in a positive way, e.g. putting their head down into the prime position, continue with a few butts to the head. If the head or arm are inaccessible, you can aim for any body part really. Be alert for bad reactions from someone engaged in an important human activity. In this case, abort 'nudge and rub' instantly and try again later. Once you've succeeded with a few head butts you can vary

the approach and throw in some head rubs, using the top and side of your head. I was able to teach G within weeks and in no time he was gently headbutting me back.

When the human responds in this manner, it's essential to purr to show your approval. This is how the training method works: you win a few pats with a head butt or two and reward the human with some sustained purring. Simple as that!

Because humans can be slow learners, they need to have messages constantly reinforced. Practise the nudge and rub as often as you can. Each and every time I interact with G or R I throw in a few head butts to remind them of their training. I even make use of the dog-like behaviours we Tonkinese are known for: I run out to greet them when they return home and, once they're seated in the lounge, I go straight for the nudge and rub.

Positive reinforcement is your friend — you can never do it too much. It's like what humans call investing in the future/money in the bank. The more you put in, the more you get back later.

The Tap Tap Method

G loves this human-esque action, perhaps above any of my other affectionate behaviours. You would be astounded how many additional pats per hour I can generate from this simple act.

Take the morning routine. G wakes up pretty late by cat standards — he's not an early morning prowler. Around 6.30 a.m., when he gets up to pee in the Big White Bowl, he will open the bedroom door, thus giving me the opportunity I need. After he's returned to bed I race in and jump up to where his sleepy head is sticking out of the bedclothes. I take one paw and tap gently on his face three or four times. At first he ignores me, but, trust me, this little act of friendship from a devoted cat is hard to resist. Soon he'll be patting me on the head and scratching me under the chin. Success! Just make sure to retract your claws when attempting this method or you risk losing at least a week's worth of training.

I heartily recommend to other felines the Tap Tap strategy I've implemented with G, which has endeared me to him and made him my closest friend. A fact that makes R visibly displeased whenever verbally acknowledged by G.

R is a very small human but has a powerful personality. Like other humans, most of her fur is on her head, a fact which continues to puzzle me. Humans

are poorly adapted to cold climates, judging by their method of adding more layers to their bodies when the temperature drops. They often have more hair in places, such as between their legs and under their arms, which are always warmer and don't really need it. If you can de-riddle this evolutionary anomaly, please do let me know. Anyway, R was quite insulted to have me, a cat, described as G's best friend. 'What do you mean

he's your best friend? What about me?' she said indignantly. It's conversations like these you will be rewarded with if you complete the training process properly.

So, here's how I apply the Tap Tap Method. If G goes into his office, as he does most days, and stares at the Shiny White Screen, I give him a tap or two. If he responds, I am satisfied that his training is working, and I'll let him get on with his human business. I will then move to sit in the sun by the window and look out, just to make sure there are no neighbourhood cats trying to sneak past. If G ignores me for too long, I will move back to sit quite close to (if not on top of) his keyboard and stare into his face.

Obstruction of human tools is a highly effective

strategy for getting affection from humans. Our little ritual goes like this: G pointedly avoids eye contact until I do a very gentle tap tap on his face, staring at him all the while. He usually chuckles and gives me a couple of strong head pats with a comment like, 'You're a good boy, Bean! Yes, you are!'

Now, cats, it's important to exploit every single opportunity to employ the Tap Tap Method. Nowhere is out of bounds — not even the Big White Bowl room, though some humans may try to make you believe otherwise. You can become quite inventive in your strategies for reaching their face so you can give them a friendly tap. I'm a big fan of jumping on the dining table so I can reach G and dispense a few face taps. Be careful with this because G allows me to do whatever I like . . . complete freedom because we're such good mates. On the other hand, R bans me from the table and if I dare jump on it while she's watching she'll shout angrily 'Get off that table, you know you're not allowed there!' Silly human, of course I'm allowed on it. Human couples do this a lot; one member of the partnership says and does one thing, while the other does something quite different. You need to factor these anomalies into their training.

G is always amused by any variation on the method

and says things like, 'You mad cat!' In fact, he once put one of my maddest escapades on Instagram as he thought it was so offbeat and funny. On the occasion in question G was in the kitchen preparing to make a coffee. I leapt up on the shiny instant cooking surface that you turn on with just a finger tap. As I landed, one of my paws turned the thing on, causing it to make a beeping noise. G turned to me and quickly took a photo. His Insta-post said 'Paws for thought: Bean can turn on the induction stove. Imagine if he toasted his paws!'

It is quite clear that he appreciates my creativity. With enough perseverance, your human will enjoy it too.

Cat Chat

Humans think they have us all figured out. It is amazing
how many articles and books have been written
about how we communicate with them. There's even
a fancy term for those who work in this field — cat
behaviourists, sometimes called 'meow experts'.

Some of you pussies hardly talk at all and you'll

need to work on that. Humans love interacting with you, especially when you are rewarding them with head butts, purring and friendly meows. They are convinced that when they speak to you and you answer back, you're communicating with them. Well, of course you are — communicating a simple message like 'hurry up and open that can' or 'go and get the cat biscuits out', but it's important to let your human imagine you're saying whatever it is they need to hear.

We Oriental breeds are well known for being big talkers. But I admit that a Siamese's long piercing cries can grate, even on cat nerves. You Siamese cats out there may want to consider toning it down a little. Tonkinese were in fact a conscious endeavour to breed a cat with a less piercing voice than the Siamese but with the loving nature and intelligence shared by the Siamese and Burmese, making us prime cat companions . . . but I digress.

Teaching your human to speak basic cat is well worth the effort. You'll need to ensure you're clear in the volume, length and tone of your meows if your humans are to follow along.

My advice is to keep your meows and body language simple. Here are some easy catversation starters that you can use with your biped:

- Short meow using a low, even tone while you make eye contact with ears and tail up = 'Hi. How's it going?'
- Repeated meows at a steady volume = 'Good to see you! What've you been doing?'
- Drawn-out, deep-voiced meeeooowww! = 'I'm starving — why haven't you given me any food yet?'
- Loud, high-pitched meow = 'Put me down, you imbecile,' or 'You've stepped on my tail, you fool!'
- Deep guttural drawn-out meow (often with a mouse or other prey in the mouth) = 'Here you are. You're welcome.'
- Grumbling, chittering-type meow = 'What do you think of the state of the current socio-economic climate?' Getting this one across has proven to be difficult and may, on second thought, be best avoided.

Of course, you have to pay attention to the other sounds you're making too. You should master purring, in particular, as that is interpreted by even the densest of humans as the sign of a happy and contented feline. At the other end of the scale is hissing, another universally understood message. This is the way to communicate anger or fear and all set to attack if the situation calls for it.

If you're looking for a bit of a laugh, you might like to read all the 'deeply analytical' things humans have written about what our body language is communicating. Here is a typical bit of human writing about cats interacting with each other: 'Eye contact is another way cats communicate with each other. If your cat looks at another cat and blinks, she is telling them through cat body language that she is receptive to their approach and attention.' (petmd.com)

Oh, humans. Not entirely wrong, of course, but so much nuance is missed. Remember, these two-legged creatures can barely read each other's body language, let alone that of another species.

The cat whisperers do sometimes, however, make accurate observations.

Here's an example: 'Cats who are hissing or growling with their backs and tails arched, their ears flattened against their heads, and their forelimbs close to their hind limbs may be on the verge of attacking. When agitated, many cats will also lash their tails from side to side.' That one is pretty obvious though.

Speaking of the cat whisperers and their so-called 'wisdom', there is one particular myth that is often bandied about willy-nilly. I'm speaking of course of the myth that cats typically have nine lives, aka nine brushes with death before they turn up their paws for real. If you believe this nonsense you are as deluded as the poor human beings who are terrified of bad luck resulting from a black cat running across their path. As a responsible human owner or manager, you need to encourage your people to treat you with as much care and attention as other pets.

Of course we do have lightning reflexes and you would have heard the phrase 'cat-like agility', right? The nine lives story presumably originated from observation of our supreme athleticism: we have flexible bones and ligaments which helps us avoid injuries in adventures that go wrong, such as falling out of trees. We are also known for a 'righting reflex' which allows us to cleverly twist so we land on our, er, landing pads.

Oh, and, by the way, we got short-changed on the nine-lives myth in some parts of the world! In certain regions of Spain we were only attributed seven lives, and Turkish legends only gave us six.

Your (Human's) Bed

There is one simple rule that you need to apply above all others when it comes to your human's bedroom — make sure you establish your position on the bed before they get there. Settle yourself comfortably in the middle of the bed. Don't position yourself to one side, as it allows your human to more easily roll you off, or climb into bed and squeeze you over to the precipice.

The human's bed is a wonderful place, full of warmth and comfort, which must remain accessible to you at all costs. Over the years I've worked up a few different tactics. On a cold morning, I run up the bed to where the top of the duvet is positioned, just under G's chin. I launch into some burrowing motions as a signal for G to lift up the duvet so I can climb under it and crawl down to around thigh level. That's where there is a big expanse of warm skin to lie against and doze for a while until one of the humans decide they really have to get up and begin their day. Perfection.

The human bed can be a dangerous place, however, especially where larger members of the species are concerned. If your human is a light sleeper with a tendency to roll from one side to the other, you can easily become trapped underneath their bulk and risk suffocation. This is the moment to remember those sharp little hooks your paws come equipped with. They are not for picking strawberries . . . unsheath 'em and give your person a quick warning rake across some delicate skin. It serves as a reminder of who is really in charge. It's crude and animalistic, I know, but a quick swipe gets results! Unlike us, humans have a low pain threshold.

So, anyway, if you've managed to assume your prime spot in the middle, a well-trained human will simply slip in beside you and shunt you a little sideways so they can fit themselves in. This may seem inconvenient, but in actual fact sharing the bed with your human, as long as you can maintain that prime position, can be an acceptable trade-off for the warmth that humans provide.

If you live with two humans who share a bed, although a bit more crowded, it can also have its benefits. Position yourself between them so that they radiate warmth from either side of you. This will also discourage any mating activities, also called 'romance', which can be disruptive to a sound sleep.

Some humans may try to prohibit your presence on the bed, believing the zone to be 'theirs'. In a case like this you will need to work at winning your human over using previously mentioned techniques (see The Tap Tap Method, p. 35 and The Nudge and Rub Method, p. 31). before they will let you stay. To avoid any risk of being ejected during the night (humans hate disturbed sleep, probably because they sleep so infrequently), sleep as quietly, and as still, as possible.

So whose bed is it? Well, it's yours, of course, but if you're a smart cat you'll be padding down the path of peaceful coexistence for the sake of all concerned.

The Living Room and Scratching Poles

Cats, you need to carefully note how much time your humans spend in their living room and how much they value the things in it. Sofas, for instance, can be strictly claw-free zones, especially if they are made of leather (a material made from the backs of large dead animals). Fun cat games, like sliding on your back under the sofa using your front claws to manoeuvre, are generally frowned upon.

Save your claws for the carpet-wrapped scratching pole your humans will usually place somewhere in their lounge. A spirited scratching of the pole will pretty much guarantee a thankful response from the nearest human: 'What a good boy!' etc. The humans think they've been quite clever by providing a structure designed for us to channel our scratching impulses. The first scratching pole was of course designed by a cat whose human sketched it out on paper before heading out to the shed to build it.

A Warning: Watch Where You Poop

Ever since humans created their first huts centuries ago, and we moved indoors with them, they've tried to teach us something they call 'house training'. In accordance with their inexplicable social rules, humans decided to hide a lot of ordinary animal behaviours, and so they began using the Big White Bowl for their waste.

Humans managed to figure out that cats like to poo in a little loose dirt after a scratch or two with hind legs, so they set out to bring the outdoors inside, you might

say. They came up with stuff they call 'cat litter'. The litter is made from materials like clay, wheat and corn. If you see what they call a litter box, filled with some strange pretend dirt, please reward the humans by peeing and pooping in it. You are guaranteed to receive extra pats and attention — an easy win!

Whatever you do, don't poop in the house. The same goes for vomiting. We throw up when we eat grass because we don't have the right enzymes to break down vegetable matter, fur, bones or feathers. Your human, though, is only concerned with keeping their house clean and will not be happy with you if you vomit inside, no matter how natural it may be.

Remember that they insist on doing all *their* excretion and vomiting in private.

Another tip before we move on: that little flap in the door set at perfect cat height is designed specifically for your usage. Your humans have probably spent lots of money installing this special 24-hour entry and exit, so do them a favour and use it. Besides, think of all the bother involved if you had to wake them up every time you wanted to go outside at night. Some wise human used robot technology to invent a personalised cat

door. This involves microchipping us so that these cat doors open only for the cat of the house — ensuring the neighbourhood cats can't get in to raid our food. Incredible! It's a shame we can't chip their big doors to keep out the people we know are not the least bit cat-friendly.

Playing 'Fetch'

Good news, youngsters: humans of all ages love kittens. It seems that a fluffy kitten sparks nurturing feelings in humans, inciting them to play all sorts of games with you. It's in your interest to play along (what delight it will bring your humans), and you will likely find you enjoy it and may want to continue such play well into your cat years.

We Tonkinese have mastered dog-like 'fetch' behaviours. But any cat can encourage their owner to throw a rolled-up piece of paper and shout, 'Fetch!' Sometimes you need to seed the idea in their rather slow brains by dropping a bit of paper or a round rubber toy at their feet, until it dawns on them that they could throw it for you to retrieve. When you return it, their faces break into beaming smiles and you receive pats galore.

Don't let dogs try to grab all the human attention, as they're inclined to do. It's time we break the stereotype of cats as 'disinterested' and claim our rightful place as human's best friend. I urge you kittens to adopt fetch behaviours as one of the many ways to endear yourselves to your humans. Don't worry about getting locked into endless games of fetch — humans have rather short attention spans and quickly tire of most games. If you've chosen your human well, they will continue to invent some new games so you don't become bored.

One of the games I've developed with G is called 'finger-nipping'. It usually takes place at night, while sitting on his lap watching TV. He will twitch a finger

to imitate a mousey movement and I respond with a quick bite and chew — never hard, just a play bite. This game can go on a long time with endless variations and is an excellent way to keep your human amused and believing they are smarter than you. Just remember to never pierce the skin, as people get upset if you draw blood (it seems an arbitrary line, I know, but remember that so many human rules are arbitrary). So, you see, once you've established you are game-ready, the possibilities are endless.

Steal Something

Theft is an activity that in human society goes against what they call a 'law'. Breaking these laws is not allowed. Cats, however, are thankfully exempt from these rules, and humans will cackle with delight when you bring home an item of clothing stolen from a neighbour's house. It can be a risky mission, but well worth the effort. Human coverings are fascinating — soft, warm, brightly coloured — there are endless variations. Especially interesting, if you can get your paws on them, are the things humans call 'underwear' — thin clothing that is normally hidden under other coverings. These are strange garments that have always puzzled me, but your human will be extra entertained if you bring some home.

A Tonkinese cousin of mine (named Tonk — original, I know) who lived with G and R for many years was a clever thief who made an art of stealing 'underwear'. Tonk had a real liking for women's underwear, often in black lace or blood-red colours. (This is part of the mystery — why do they bother with bold colours and intricate designs when they are covered up under other clothes?) But he was a true master of the craft and knew the importance of variation, bringing in T-shirts, socks and toys, just to keep the humans on their toes.

Stealing seems to be a Tonkinese trait (though it really is good fun, and I'd encourage all cats to try it at least once). A fellow Tonkinese named Brigit from Hamilton, New Zealand, became internationally renowned for stealing underwear, snaffling 11 pairs of men's boxers in only two months. An amazing feat we should all aspire to. She also collected 50 pairs of socks and liked to steal them in pairs, prioritising organisation; a cat after my own heart.

Hunting

Most of us hunt enthusiastically. It's what we do and have done since the beginning of time. As you will soon find out, however, humans become strangely disturbed when we bring home prey. I've come to understand it is because, in their eyes, we've abruptly morphed from cute kitty to ruthless killer. Suddenly, they are disappointed with us; we've let them down. They will forgive you eventually but it's probably a good idea not to overdo it in the hunting department.

Insects are fair game — humans don't seem to mind so much if we kill those, so long as we don't make too much of a mess. But birds are a real problem, especially the ones

humans call 'endangered'. It means there are not many of them left.

Remember Tibbles who wiped out the Stephens Island wren? Humans are eager for such 'atrocities' not to happen again, so they hate it when we bring home one of these 'special' birds, especially if we start dismembering it in front of them.

Humans have a weird double standard, don't they? We know how many chickens they eat — so, what's so different about eating other birds?

Just because they don't catch their prey themselves, it doesn't make them any different from us. It's like they're in denial about being carnivores. My theory is that humans have become so divorced from their instincts that they've forgotten the thrill of the chase.

Humans also dislike mice. They can react with incomprehensible fear when we bring the precious gift of a field mouse inside the house, caught with incredible speed and skill, especially if it's still alive, or half alive. Don't be offended when your human doesn't appreciate the trouble you went to — it's pitiable, really, that they can no longer experience the excitement and pride that comes with the hunt.

Humans have no understanding of one of our favourite games: Juggle the Mouse. You know what

I'm talking about — the unparalleled joy of repeatedly tossing a field mouse into the air and catching it. The game gets even more exciting if the said rodent is still alive and is fit enough to make a bolt for safety while we give chase. Your human may scold you or try to free the mouse, and you would be wise to take your meal outside if you wish to continue the game.

Dogs

These slobbering, smelly, undisciplined, lumbering creatures have long been called 'man's best friend'. Mystifying, really. Especially seeing as they are often a cat's worst enemy. It's up to you to teach your human that the friendship from a feline can far surpass that of some mangy mutt.

In a worst-case scenario you may have to share your home with a dog. It sounds horrifying, I know, but don't despair if your human brings a dog home. Just hold your ground and hopefully the dog will fall into line.

The first thing you must do is establish the pecking order. First impressions really count — you must assert your dominance straight away, and the only way to do this is to attack ferociously. You have claws for a reason, so use them! Remember that you are the head of the household, with humans next in the order and dogs right at the bottom. When G and R allowed their son's dog, Elwood, into the house, I launched a fierce attack on him, screeching, spitting and clawing. The dog was taken by surprise and immediately rolled onto his back, accepting the subservient position with almost no fuss.

Sharing all the good things, such as a warm spot in front of the heater, can be achieved without having to fight tooth and claw. Some modern dogs (they come in lots of strange mutant breeds like the labradoodle these days) are oddly tolerant of cats, and with these variants attack methods aren't even necessary. These dogs go about their business and hardly acknowledge our presence. The most tolerant can even provide a warm place to lie on their large, furry stomachs. Indeed, once you've established your relationship with the dog, you might find they have their uses.

Cats Rule Online

Cats are masterful influencers. Our success online is
a tribute to every single feline who has starred on
YouTube, Instagram, Facebook and other social media
platforms. Images and videos of cats make up some of
the most viewed content on the Internet. There is even

a book written for humans called *How to Make Your Cat an Internet Celebrity: A Guide to Financial Freedom*.

The success of cats on the Internet proves just how much joy we bring to the lives of humans. It has been estimated that cats drive almost 15 percent of all web traffic and there are 30 million Google searches per month for the term 'cat'. When G checked out 'the funniest cat videos' on the Internet, something called 'Funny Cat Compilation' had received over 31 million views. Humans really can't get enough of us.

Many an Internet-savvy feline has lined the cat hall of fame over the years. Grumpy Cat was one of the biggest Internet sensations — a sour-faced puss, real name Tardar Sauce, that went viral in 2012. The Arizona cat that 'helped millions of people smile' ended up with more than two million Instagram followers and countless memes (oh the memes!) before her tragic passing at the tender age of seven in 2019.

Cats have also been the inspiration behind much human creativity. Nyan Cat, a Japanese cartoon creation, was another smash hit online, while a whole subculture of memes sprouted around the idea of the Lolcat — the language used in these memes has even come to be known as 'Lolspeak' or 'Kitty Pidgin!'

As you can see, the golden age of cats is far from

over, with tributes to our glory existing in cities all over the world. Amsterdam loves its cats, with cat-themed attractions like De Poezenboot (The Cat Boat), a shelter for cats on a converted houseboat that is home to about 17 cats. Amsterdam's KattenKabinet is a museum devoted to art featuring cats. It has a collection of paintings, sculptures, photos, prints and furniture, including works by the likes of Picasso and Rembrandt (both well-known cat lovers).

Every single one of you cats has a part to play in maintaining our Internet profile. Unfortunately, I'm a bit too old to become an influencer, so I'll leave the Gramming and TikToking to you kittens. Amp up the cuteness at every opportunity when your humans are present, inspiring them to get their phones out and snap a photo or video of you playing with boxes, cat toys, paper, almost anything! Stay alert for every possible opportunity to become a star. Always photo bomb a human's selfie. You'll need to be alert at all times for the right moment to jump into the shot, and try to contort your face into some strange expression for maximum entertainment value. You can also try sleeping in an odd location, or in a cute pose with your paws wrapped around your face (scientifically proven to be irresistible to humans).

And there you have it. With that last piece of advice, I pass the torch on to you, my kittens, in the hope that you will go on to become successful human-trainers, companions, and maybe even celebrities. It's a tough life being a cat (being this perfect has its challenges), but with this book as your guide, I have no doubt you will go on to help cats take their rightful place as rulers of the world.

Sadly, Bean passed away from kidney disease in 2020, shortly after he finished writing this book.

References

Carlin, P 2014, *How to Make Your Cat an Internet Celebrity: A Guide to Financial Freedom*, Quirk Books, Philadelphia.

Darton, R 2009, *The Great Cat Massacre and Other Episodes in French Cultural History*, Barnes & Noble, Basic Books, New York.

Haddon, C 2019, *A Cat's Guide to Humans, From A to Z*, by George the Cat, owner of Celia Haddon, Hodder & Stoughton.

Websites

Anon. 2016, 'Cat Burglar Prefers to Take Underwear', viewed
September 2019, <www.nzherald.co.nz>

Fouchi Esneault M 2016, 'The Power of Purr', <www.mcall.com>

Harvey C 2014, 'The Crazy Story of a Cat Named Tibbles
Who Killed Off a Whole Species of Bird', viewed July 2019,
<businessinsider.com.au>

Haddon C, *Understanding Animals Through Their Behaviour*,
viewed July 2019, <catexpert.co.uk>

Simon's Cat, viewed September 2019, <www.simonscat.com>

Sung W 2018, 'Cat Language 101: How Do Cats Talk to Each
Other', viewed August 2019, <www.petmd.com>

Taylor A 2014, 'Swiss Under Pressure to Ban the Eating of Dogs
and Cats', <www.washingtonpost.com>

The Catboat (De Poezenboot), Amsterdam, Netherlands,
viewed August 2019, <www.depoezenboot.nl>

The Cat Cabinet Museum (KattenKabinet), Amsterdam,
Netherlands, viewed August 2019, <www.kattenkabinet.nl>

The Official Home of Hello Kitty and Friends, viewed
September 2019, <www.sanrio.com>